Speak Up, Start Now

Rosa Hart

Design and Publishing Support: Global Bookshelves International, LLC

ISBN: 979-8-218-82009-1

Published by: Rosa Hart Media Consulting, LLC

To comment on this eBook, send an email to the author at info@nurserosaspeaks.com.

Notice

The author has made every effort to ensure the accuracy and completeness of the information presented in this book. However, the author cannot be held responsible for the continued currency of the information, any inadvertent errors, or the application of this information to practice. Therefore, the author shall have no liability to any person or entity with regard to claims, loss, or damage caused or alleged to be caused, directly or indirectly, by the use of the information contained herein.

Table of Contents

CHAPTER 1

The Permission You're Waiting For Doesn't Exist

Hey there, nurses. Let's have a real talk. How many times have you been told that to truly advance in this field, you need more letters after your name? Want to climb that career ladder? Time to get an MSN! Dreaming of teaching? Doctorate, please! Yearning for that sweet, sweet autonomy? Hello, Nurse Practitioner program! It feels like every path leads back to the classroom, right?

But here's the thing: what if we're so busy chasing those credentials that we miss the bigger picture? What if the real question isn't "What degree do I need?" but "What impact do

I want to make?" We put so much pressure on ourselves to be perfectly qualified, to have all the answers before we even open our mouths. But what if that's exactly what's holding us back?

The Weight of Nursing

If you've worked at the bedside, you never forget the feeling after a shift. It seeps into your bones—the weight of responsibility, the emotional residue of witnessing life and death up close. It's not just physical exhaustion; it's a profound weariness that lingers long after you've clocked out.

I remember cradling a tiny NICU baby, their little body wracked with tremors from opioid withdrawal. Their back arched in a way I didn't know was possible, and I was struck by the fragility of their existence. It made me question my own assumptions about parenthood and the silent struggles so many families face.

And the ICU? Eight years in that environment showed me the profound weight of our profession. I can still vividly recall the patient who needed six of us to reposition him, the constant beeping of machines, the alarms that seemed to echo long after my shift ended. One particularly difficult shift, the bariatric bed actually broke under the weight of this patient as we tried to turn him. We scrambled to find another bed, all while trying to maintain his dignity and prevent skin breakdown. Those sounds, those experiences, they stay with you. They shape you.

The Credential Trap

It's easy to get caught in the trap of thinking those experiences aren't enough. We're conditioned to believe that without more letters after our names, our options are limited. School nursing, management, teaching—all those paths seem to require another degree, another certification.

I remember those break room conversations, nurses huddled together, scarfing down snacks between shifts, venting about the demands of the job. Inevitably, someone would mention going back to school, as if it were the only way out. But that kind of thinking creates a false dichotomy: burn out at the bedside or go into debt chasing more credentials.

I found myself falling into that trap too. I remember sitting at my dining room table, researching advocacy work with the American Heart Association, and feeling wholly inadequate. Everyone testifying before Congress seemed to have a doctorate. "Who's going to listen to me if I'm 'just a nurse'?" I thought.

My husband, in his infinite wisdom, pointed out that the most compelling speakers aren't always the most educated. They're the ones who can connect with people, who can weave data and emotion into a story that resonates. He encouraged me to trust my own experiences, to find my voice, and to share my story.

From Homeschooling to Stroke Certification: Unconventional Paths to Expertise

His words resonated with me, reminding me of my own unconventional upbringing. Growing up homeschooled with five siblings, our kitchen table transformed daily into a classroom. My mom, with her music education degree and impeccable handwriting, instilled in me a love of learning that extended far beyond textbooks. She used a distinctive yellow-edged book with lines above the long 'a' sounds to teach me to read, and her handwriting was so perfect it looked like a font. Every Friday, we'd visit the library, a place where I devoured books, meticulously maintaining a handwritten list that, by sixth grade, boasted over 2,000 titles.

My mom had this incredible knack for turning everyday moments into teachable moments. We'd watch Star Trek and discuss Uhura's groundbreaking role as a Black woman on television, or we'd explore the science behind why salt melts snow. She taught me that learning happens everywhere, not just within the confines of a traditional classroom. We didn't always have dedicated teachers for every subject, and interruptions from siblings were a constant. But my mom, with her unwavering belief in our potential, made it work.

That early independence served me well, especially when it came time for college. I navigated the application process, secured financial aid, and paved my own path—all without the guidance of a guidance counselor. I remember studying for the ACT with a friend, determined to earn a good score so I could qualify for scholarships. And it paid off—I received enough financial aid to cover my tuition and even help my husband pay for his master's in teaching.

Years later, when my mentor, Lynn Hundley, encouraged me to pursue my Stroke Certified Registered Nurse (SCRN) certification, I hesitated. Lynn, a force of nature who built our stroke program from the ground up, had this incredible ability to command respect, even without a doctorate. She had this infectious passion and dedication that drew people in, and she saw something in me, a potential I hadn't fully recognized.

"Rosa," she'd say, "you have a knack for this. You need to share your knowledge." She believed in the power of certification, not just for the letters after your name, but for the validation it provided. Lynn herself had been instrumental in writing the SCRN exam, and she knew firsthand how important it was to the profession to have nurses who were recognized experts in stroke care.

With her encouragement, I took the plunge. I studied diligently, attending the review classes twice, determined to master the material. The exam itself took place in the most unlikely of settings—a cramped cubicle in what looked like an H&R Block office. But that experience, as bizarre as it was, solidified something important for me: true expertise comes from experience, not just a setting or a piece of paper.

Lynn's legacy, tragically cut short by glioblastoma in 2023, served as a powerful reminder that impact transcends titles. It took six people to fill the void she left—a testament to the profound difference she made by building something meaningful from the ground up. She taught me that you don't need a doctorate to make a national, even global, impact. You just need passion, dedication, and the willingness to share your knowledge with the world.

Finding My Voice, One Conversation at a Time

Think about this: cardiovascular disease is the number one killer in our country, yet only 2% of NIH funding goes to cardiovascular research. That's a staggering statistic, and it highlights a critical need for nurses to advocate for our patients and our profession. Maybe your passion lies elsewhere—patient education, improving nurse staffing ratios, advocating for better mental health support. Whatever it is, your voice matters.

I've always been drawn to connection—that spark when you truly see and hear another person. It's about reading between the lines, sensing the unspoken questions, and diving deeper. During the pandemic, that human connection felt miles away. Podcasting became my lifeline, a way to bridge the distance and share stories that mattered. It wasn't about having all the answers or being a polished expert; it was about creating a space for authentic conversations.

The Power of Decisiveness

Here's the thing about impact: it rarely waits for the perfect moment or the perfectly crafted plan. Being decisive doesn't mean you have all the answers; it means you're willing to take action with the knowledge you have right now. At the bedside, we don't hesitate to act when a patient crashes. We don't wait for permission to advocate for what's right. We trust our instincts and we move forward.

I've learned to approach decisions with a "decide and see how you feel" mentality. It's not about being reckless, but about trusting your gut and being open to adjusting course along the way. When I started podcasting, I didn't have a fancy setup or a detailed plan. I just knew I wanted to connect with people and share their stories. That initial leap of faith, that willingness to try, has led to some of the most rewarding experiences of my career.

Redefining Expertise

In the academic world, there's a lot of focus on book smarts over real-world know-how. But the most valuable insights often come from nurses who've spent years in the trenches—problem-solving, finding workarounds, and advocating for their patients. I've seen nurses with a string of certifications struggle to handle situations that require quick thinking and adaptability. Experience, I've learned, is its own form of expertise.

I'm not saying education isn't valuable. It absolutely is. But waiting for more credentials before making an impact? That's a form of self-sabotage. Your experience matters. Your perspective matters. Your voice matters—right now, not after your next certification.

Reflection Questions

1. What personal experiences have shaped your understanding of the nursing profession beyond formal education?
2. How do you define the impact you want to make in your career, and what steps can you take to achieve it without waiting for additional credentials?
3. Can you recall a moment when you felt your voice or perspective was undervalued due to a lack of formal qualifications? How did you handle it?
4. In what ways can you leverage your unique experiences to advocate for change or improvement in your field?
5. How can you cultivate decisiveness in your professional life, and what small actions can you take today to start making a difference?

Action Steps

- Identify one area where your current experience gives you unique insights. What are you passionate about? What problems have you encountered that you're uniquely positioned to address?

- Write down three ways you could share your expertise without additional credentials. This could be anything from starting a blog or podcast to mentoring a colleague or volunteering in your community.
- Find one opportunity this week to speak up about something you care about. This could be as simple as sharing an article on social media, writing a letter to the editor, or starting a conversation with a colleague.
- Connect with someone who's making an impact in your field and ask about their journey. You'll be amazed by how many people are willing to share their stories and offer guidance.

Remember: The healthcare system needs your voice now. Your experiences, your insights, your perspective—these are valuable right now, not after your next set of letters. The only permission you need to make a difference is your own. Don't wait to be perfect. Don't wait to be "ready." Start where you are, with what you know, and let your impact grow from there. Because the truth is, the permission you're waiting for doesn't exist—and that's exactly why you need to start now.

CHAPTER 2

Finding My Voice in the ICU

When people ask about my nursing career, they often expect tales of dramatic saves or heroic moments. And sure, there were plenty of those in the ICU. But what truly shaped me during my eight years in critical care weren't the adrenaline-filled emergencies—it was the quiet transformations that happened in between. Working in critical care changed not just how I practiced nursing, but how I viewed the world and found my voice as an advocate.

The Journey to Critical Care

My path to the ICU wasn't a straight line. It actually started with a detour—a detour that involved a positive pregnancy test and a sudden realization that maybe, just maybe, I was meant to be a nurse. It was my junior year of college, and I was taking anatomy and physiology "for fun." I found myself engrossed in the intricacies of the human body, fascinated by how everything worked together. And get this—I was getting better grades than the nursing students! That's when the thought first crossed my mind: "Wait, maybe I should be a nurse."

That summer, while pregnant with my son, my paternal grandfather, Papa, had a heart attack. I remember visiting him in the ICU, feeling a mix of fear and awe. I'd never really been around serious medical situations before, and seeing the doctors and nurses working together to save his life was both terrifying and inspiring. The cardiologist even showed us the images of the stents he'd placed in Papa's heart, explaining how they'd opened up the blockages. It was like witnessing a miracle unfold right before my eyes.

That experience, coupled with my newfound love for anatomy and physiology, solidified my decision. I enrolled in nursing school at Jefferson Community and Technical College, eager to learn everything I could about this profession that had captivated me. Initially, I dreamed of becoming a flight nurse, so I took a position as a unit secretary in the ICU to get my foot in the door. From there, I became a nurse's aide, floating between different ICU units while completing my studies.

It was during those early experiences, caring for those incredibly vulnerable NICU babies in the pediatric rotation of nursing school, that the weight of the work first struck me. I remember holding one tiny baby, their body trembling uncontrollably from opioid withdrawal. Their back contorted in a way I didn't think possible, and I was overwhelmed by the thought of their suffering. It made me realize how much I had to learn about the complexities of healthcare and the silent battles so many face.

As I continued working as an aide, I found myself drawn to the neuro nursing units. The nurses there just clicked with my personality and approach to patient care. I came from a background that emphasized natural remedies over medical interventions. My family prioritized supplements over medications, and I brought that idealistic perspective with me. But the ICU quickly taught me that while preventive care has its place, there are times when only immediate medical intervention can save a life.

The Reality of Critical Care

Like many new nurses, I started with a sort of savior complex, believing I could fix everything if I just tried hard enough. The ICU had other plans. Every day at work was the worst day of someone's life. You're not just dealing with critical illness—you're confronting human suffering in its rawest form.

Most nights, as a nursing aide, I was responsible for floating among five different ICU units. Death, as they say, comes in threes, and our units were no exception. I found myself performing postmortem care on three patients, each loss a heavy weight on my heart. But amidst the grief, there were moments of intense action, situations that tested my limits and ignited a passion for the unpredictable nature of critical care.

I remember one particularly chaotic shift. A patient, confused and disoriented, had gotten out of bed and attempted to use the bathroom. He had C. diff, and the result was a scene straight out of a horror movie—diarrhea splattered across the walls, the floor, the toilet. I was alone, covered in sweat and isolation gear, desperately trying to clean up the mess before shift change. The smell of bleach wipes filled the air, a pungent reminder of the less glamorous side of nursing.

Then there was the woman who had swallowed a bag of meth, causing a massive GI bleed. I held pressure on her abdomen, blood soaking through my gloves and dripping onto my shoes. Another nurse tried to wipe my shoes clean, but I waved her off. “Let’s just focus on stopping the bleeding,” I said, adrenaline coursing through my veins. The chaos, the urgency, the sheer intensity of the situation—it was both terrifying and exhilarating.

These experiences, as messy and challenging as they were, solidified my love for the ICU. I wasn’t fazed by blood or bodily fluids. I thrived in the fast-paced environment, where quick thinking and decisive action were essential. I realized that I wasn’t an adrenaline junkie, per se, but I was drawn to the challenge, the constant learning, the opportunity to make a real difference in people’s lives.

Working in the ICU forces you to accept hard truths. Sometimes, despite everyone’s best efforts and prayers, patients don’t survive. Sometimes there aren’t clear solutions or happy endings. And sometimes, the suffering you witness has nothing to do with poor choices—it's simply the reality of a healthcare system that doesn't serve everyone equally.

These realizations changed me. I went from someone who always needed to be right, who believed there were rational arguments for everything, to someone who understood that comfort and compassion often matter more than being correct. When you're surrounded by suffering every day, you start to care less about winning arguments and more about easing pain—whether physical or emotional.

The Angel of Death (With a Heart of Gold)

Over time, I developed a reputation in the ICU. They started calling me the "Angel of Death," but not for the reason you might think. I became the go-to nurse for end-of-life and hospice cases because I wasn't afraid of the emotional weight they carried. Other nurses would call me to help with distressed family members: "Can you please hug their family member so they'll stay out of the way?"

They'd say I was "better than drugs" because I could often calm people down without medication. This wasn't some special talent—it came from learning to truly listen and validate people's fears and concerns. When someone's loved one is critically ill, they don't always need solutions. Sometimes they just need someone who isn't afraid to sit with them in their pain.

Learning to Lead Through Listening

One of the most valuable lessons I learned came from working with the interdisciplinary team at our comprehensive stroke center. During my BSN program, we talked extensively about interdisciplinary care, but seeing it in action was different. Every morning, we'd have rounds with neurology, pharmacy, physical therapy, occupational therapy, speech therapy, case management, social work, dietary—the whole team coming together for our stroke patients.

I learned tremendously from mentors like Dr. Gauhar Chaudhary, who patiently taught me how to improve my neuro assessments. My nurse educator, Annette Matangi, emphasized the importance of getting patients mobile as soon as possible to prevent delirium. I prioritized having patients alert and ready for therapy, coordinated with music therapy for anxiety management, and worked closely with chaplains to help families navigate difficult decisions about healthcare surrogates.

I remember going into patient rooms with the physical therapists, eager to learn their techniques and understand their perspective. I'd help mobilize patients on ventilators, carefully detaching IV lines and monitoring their vitals as they took their first tentative steps. I shadowed speech therapists and occupational therapists, fascinated by their ability to assess cognitive function and help patients regain lost skills.

These interdisciplinary rounds weren't just about sharing information; they were about building relationships, fostering trust, and creating a shared sense of purpose. We were all there for the patient, working together to provide the best possible care.

The Rhythm of Hospital Life

The ICU runs 24/7, and I experienced it from every angle. Night shift had its own culture—less administrative oversight meant we could focus purely on patient care. “Keep everybody alive till morning” was our mantra, and we did whatever it took to make that happen. Weekend shifts became my favorite; there was less politics and more camaraderie.

But this schedule came with real challenges. Holiday shifts meant missing family gatherings in Tennessee. Sometimes my husband would take the kids without me, and we’d wait until the last minute to see if I’d get “budgeted” (their term for having enough staff coverage) before making any plans. Working six days a week to save for a Disney World trip taught me hard lessons about burnout.

The Personal Cost of Caring

Let’s be honest about something they don’t teach you in nursing school: this work takes a toll. The constant state of high alert, the alarm fatigue, the missed meals, the holiday shifts—it affects you physically and emotionally. I remember getting home after 14-hour shifts, shaking from low blood sugar, trying to explain to my family why I needed to eat before I could be present for them.

Balancing motherhood with ICU nursing brought its own challenges. When my daughter was born, I was determined to continue breastfeeding while working night shifts. This meant not getting more than four consecutive hours of sleep for an entire year. I pumped on my way to work, on my way home. I alternated between using a Medela pump with yellow flanges, to a Spectra S2 that was small and pink, because it was quieter for nighttime pumping. I joined La Leche League on Facebook, connecting with other breastfeeding moms and finding solace in their shared experiences. I even donated 100 ounces of breast milk to The Milk Bank, knowing it would help nourish fragile NICU babies.

I felt this immense pressure to do it all—be a great nurse, a devoted mother, a supportive wife. But the lack of sleep was relentless. I was constantly on edge, my anxiety spilling over into every aspect of my life. Every headache felt like a potential stroke. Every time my kids played outside, I envisioned worst-case scenarios. I even found myself doing NIH Stroke Scale assessments on myself in the mirror. Eventually, this pushed me to transition to day shift—a change that ultimately led me to the comprehensive stroke center where my advocacy journey would begin.

The anxiety followed me home. Witnessing so much suffering left me struggling to find hope in everyday moments. I see echoes of my anxiety in my son, seven years older than my daughter, when he spirals into worst-case scenario thinking. While his cautiousness reassures me, it also saddens me to think I may have passed on that burden. But it's pushed me to teach him the coping strategies I've learned: focusing not just on what's possible, but what's probable.

Finding My Voice Through Experience

What I discovered through those eight years was that expertise isn't just about credentials—it's about lived experience. Every difficult conversation, every interdisciplinary success, every family we supported through end-of-life care—these experiences shaped not just how I practiced nursing, but how I viewed my role in healthcare.

Yes, I was proud when I was nominated for nurse of the year for my work with the interdisciplinary team. But what mattered more was realizing that my voice—shaped by years of bedside experience—had value. I didn't need more degrees or certifications to advocate for better patient care. The expertise I gained through direct patient care was valid and valuable.

I remember feeling frustrated in nursing school. We'd be learning the "ideal" way to do things, studying for the NCLEX, but it often felt disconnected from the realities of the ICU. I'd think, "That's a nice answer, but it wouldn't work in the real world." I learned to trust my instincts, to act quickly when needed, because in the ICU, hesitation can have dire consequences.

Bridging to Reflection and Action

As I reflect on my journey, it's clear that the lessons learned in the ICU extend far beyond the hospital walls. They've shaped my approach to life, teaching me the value of resilience, empathy, and the power of a well-timed pause. These experiences have not only defined my career but have also influenced my personal growth and understanding of what it means to truly care for others.

With these insights in mind, I invite you to consider your own journey. How have your experiences shaped your perspective? What unique insights have you gained that could benefit others? Let's explore these questions together, as we move into the reflection and action steps.

Reflection Questions

1. What experiences in your healthcare career have challenged your initial expectations or beliefs?
2. How do you currently balance emotional involvement with professional boundaries?
3. What unique perspectives has your clinical experience given you that could benefit others?
4. How has your work affected your worldview and relationships outside of healthcare?

Action Steps

- Start documenting your clinical experiences and insights (while maintaining HIPAA compliance).

- Identify one area where your expertise could contribute to improving patient care.
- Practice sharing your professional experiences with colleagues in a structured setting.
- Develop your own toolkit of coping strategies for managing work-related stress.
- Remember: Your experience matters. The insights you've gained through direct patient care are valuable, and you don't need additional credentials to start making a difference. The permission you're waiting for already exists in the expertise you've developed through your daily work.

Next time you find yourself thinking "I need more training before I can speak up," remember that your firsthand experience gives you a perspective that no textbook can provide. The healthcare system needs your voice—not someday, but now.

CHAPTER 3

The Power of Human Connection

When I think about what matters most in the work I do, it always comes back to one thing: connection. Real, human connection—the kind that makes you feel seen, heard, and valued. Whether it's sitting across from someone in an interview or catching a moment of shared understanding in the chaos of everyday life, it's those connections that truly stick with me.

Why Eye Contact Matters More Than Social Media Likes

In today's world, likes, shares, and followers often seem like the ultimate measure of success. But for me, they've never compared to the power of eye contact. There's something irreplaceable about being present with someone—seeing their facial expressions, picking up on the unspoken cues, and knowing when to ask the next question that takes the conversation deeper.

During the pandemic, that kind of connection felt especially distant. I'm a people person—I thrive on meeting new people and hearing their stories—so staying in a bubble with just my husband, kids, and a few close friends was tough. Podcasting became my lifeline during this time. I started it in July 2020 as a way to connect with others in meaningful ways, even when in-person interaction wasn't possible. But as soon as it was safe to meet people face-to-face again, I realized how much I'd missed the energy of being in the same room.

That's why I've always preferred in-person interviews. When I'm sitting across from someone, I can sense when there's more to their story—when a pause or a glance says, "Ask me about this." Those moments of intuition are harder to capture on a Zoom call, where body language gets lost in the frame. There's a connection that comes from being fully present, and it's something we're all starved for.

Creating Meaningful Conversations That Cut Through the Fluff

One thing podcasting has taught me is how to move past surface-level small talk. When you meet someone for the first time, it's easy to default to the basics: "What do you do?" "Where are you from?" But those questions rarely lead to the kind of connection I'm looking for.

Instead, I've learned to lean into curiosity. I'll never forget the time an Uber driver asked if I was interrogating her because I kept asking questions. She told me she used to be a police officer, and I think that's what sparked her reaction. I wasn't trying to be intrusive—I genuinely wanted to know more about her life and what had led her to that moment. It's that same curiosity that drives my podcast interviews, where I try to create a space where people feel comfortable opening up.

It's not just about asking questions; it's about listening. Real listening. The kind where you're not just waiting for your turn to talk but fully engaged in what the other person is saying. It's about following up with thoughtful questions and showing that you care about their answers.

Those are the conversations that stick with you long after the microphones are turned off.

Building Connections Through Shared Passions

The Lou Review podcast began during the pandemic as a way to connect with our community and support local restaurants. We visited locally owned spots, talked about what was safe to eat out, and highlighted the safety precautions they were taking. But as we got to know the restaurant owners, we realized the real magic was in their stories.

I love business owners. Their energy and passion are infectious. It's inspiring to meet people who believe in what they're doing, even when it doesn't make sense to anyone else. Like the two UofL students who started Manic Macarons. They created macarons inspired by mental health issues to spark conversations about important topics. Or the leaders of nonprofits like Apron, Inc., who provide grants to restaurant workers in crisis, and the Kentuckiana Stroke Association, who educate the community about recognizing the signs of a stroke.

These connections have shown me the power of storytelling. It's not just about sharing facts or promoting a cause; it's about making people feel something. When you tell a story, you invite others into your world. You create a bridge between your experiences and theirs, and that's where the real connection happens.

The Value of Preserving Stories Through Podcasting

Podcasting isn't just about conversations; it's about preserving stories. It's a way to capture moments and voices that might otherwise be lost. It's also a place where vulnerability and connection thrive. I remember being a guest on a podcast and sharing my story of miscarriage—an experience so personal and painful it felt almost impossible to put into words. But sharing it wasn't just cathartic for me; it created space for someone else to share her story of loss as well. That moment reminded me that connection isn't just about asking the right questions; it's about being brave enough to share a part of yourself, even when it's hard.

As a nurse, I've learned that the hardest conversations are often the ones where words feel inadequate. Listening without trying to equate stories isn't just important—it's essential. It's about holding space for someone else's pain, without rushing to fill the silence with comparisons or solutions. Not every experience needs to be matched or compared to be valid. In podcasting, this same principle holds true. By balancing listening and sharing, we create a space where others feel safe to open up.

Connection in a Lonely World

That's the power of storytelling: it reminds us that we're not alone. In a world where loneliness is increasingly recognized as a public health issue, podcasts offer a sense of connection. Listeners feel like they're part of the conversation, even if they're just sitting quietly on the other side of the headphones.

Social media may give us quick hits of dopamine, but it's real human connection—the kind that comes from eye contact, shared stories, and genuine empathy—that feeds our need for oxytocin, the "connection hormone." Think about the difference between scrolling past hundreds of Instagram likes and having one meaningful, unhurried conversation. One is fleeting, while the other leaves a lasting impact. Podcasts bridge this gap by fostering moments of intimacy and understanding, both for the hosts and the listeners who feel a part of their dialogue.

This is why connection doesn't require perfection; it just requires showing up with curiosity, empathy, and a willingness to engage. Storytelling invites people into shared spaces of vulnerability and trust, breaking down the walls we often build to protect ourselves. By sharing a piece of your own humanity—whether it's through a personal story, a thoughtful question, or even a moment of silence to truly listen—you inspire others to open up. That ripple effect can create connections that change lives, sometimes in ways you may never fully see or understand. And in a world that often feels fragmented, isn't that connection exactly what we need most?

Reflection Questions

1. How can you create deeper connections in your daily interactions, whether at work or in your personal life?

2. What stories from your own life could you share to build empathy and connection with others?
3. How has listening—without comparing or equating—helped you honor someone else's experience?

Action Steps

- Identify one person you'd like to connect with more deeply this week and reach out to them.
- Practice asking open-ended questions in your next conversation, and focus on listening without interruption.
- Think of one story from your life that has shaped who you are. Consider sharing it with someone who might benefit from hearing it.

CHAPTER 4

Starting Before You're Ready

We've all been there—staring at a new opportunity and hesitating, wondering if we're ready to take the leap. What if it doesn't work out? What if you make a mistake? What if you're just not ready? These questions can paralyze us, stopping us from even taking the first step. But here's the truth: you'll never feel completely ready. The only way to know if something will work is to start.

As an ICU nurse, I've always had to balance planning ahead with the ability to adapt in an instant. It's a skill that has shaped the way I approach starting something new: not waiting until everything feels perfect, but trusting that I can adjust as I go. It's a mindset that's shaped my approach to everything from starting a podcast to planning family vacations on a tight budget. And while I've always been a decisive person, I've learned that it's okay to change your mind along the way. Deciding isn't about committing forever - it's about giving yourself the chance to see how you feel and adjust as needed.

How to Overcome the Fear of "Messing Up"

Fear of making mistakes. It's the thing that keeps so many of us stuck, like sitting on the couch watching life happen instead of getting up and seeing what's out there. But mistakes aren't failures, they're opportunities to learn and adapt. When I first started travel hacking - that is, using credit card points and miles to save on travel - I didn't have a clue where to begin. There were points systems, fine print, and rules that made my head spin, but I figured I'd just dive in and figure it out along the way.

That decision led to one of the best family vacations we've ever had—a nearly free trip to San Diego, with flights and hotels covered by points and miles. We visited the zoo, explored museums, and even enjoyed some time by the beach. None of it would have happened if I'd waited until I knew all the answers. I gave myself the flexibility to adjust along the way, like booking flights with points that could be refunded if plans changed.

The same principle applies to so many areas of life: when you give yourself room to course-correct, starting becomes less intimidating.

Why Being a Starter Matters More Than Being a Perfect Finisher

Starting something doesn't mean you're locked into it forever. It means giving yourself the chance to explore, to see if it's a good fit. When I began podcasting, I didn't know if it would work out. I didn't have professional equipment or a clear vision for the long term. What I did have was curiosity and the willingness to try. And while I've refined my approach over time, the lessons I learned from those early episodes have shaped everything I do now.

Starting is more important than finishing perfectly because you can't finish what you don't begin. It's easy to get caught up in what the end result might look like, but the truth is, you can't predict the journey until you're on it. Some projects will blossom into something amazing; others might fizzle out. But every attempt teaches you something valuable.

Making Decisions Without Certainty

Deciding to try something new often feels risky. What if it's the wrong choice? What if it doesn't work out? Here's the thing: indecision doesn't protect you from failure—it just guarantees that nothing changes. I've learned to approach decisions with the mindset of "decide and see how you feel."

This approach isn't about being reckless; it's about being open. It means saying yes to opportunities with the understanding that you can reevaluate later. Whether it's trying a new restaurant, starting a craft project, or launching a podcast, you won't know if it's right for you until you try. And if it turns out not to be the right fit? That's okay. You can pivot, adjust, or try something else.

Decide and See How You Feel: A Simple Method to Take Action

This method has become my go-to for tackling decisions—big or small. It's not about getting everything perfect from the start; it's about moving forward and adapting along the way. Here's how it works:

1. Start by deciding, even if you feel unsure or hesitant.
2. Once you decide, take note of how you feel—excited, relieved, or maybe uneasy?
3. Let your reaction guide your next step. If it feels right, keep going. If it doesn't, adjust.

When I first started podcasting, I didn't have fancy equipment or a clear plan. But after recording the first episode, I felt a surge of energy—a sense of purpose that told me I was onto something. That feeling became my compass, encouraging me to keep going.

This method isn't about ensuring success—it's about ensuring growth. There have been times I've said yes to opportunities that didn't feel right in hindsight. But those weren't failures—they were lessons that helped me course-correct.

The beauty of the "Decide and See How You Feel" method is its simplicity. It empowers you to start, to experiment, and to learn from every step. Whether it's launching a creative project, stepping into a new role, or deciding how to spend your time, this approach encourages curiosity and courage. You don't have to be reckless to be bold—you just have to trust yourself enough to begin.

This method has become a cornerstone of how I make decisions, and it's something I've relied on time and time again. At its heart, it's about trusting yourself enough to take action, even when you don't have all the answers. Here's how it works:

Choose something—anything—and then notice how you feel. Does it light you up or weigh you down? That emotional response will show you the way.

I've applied this method to decisions big and small. When I started podcasting, I didn't know if it would work or if anyone would even listen. But after recording my first episode, that feeling of "Yes, this is it" carried me through the uncertainties that followed.

I've also made decisions that didn't sit well afterward. Instead of seeing them as failures, I treated them as feedback—a chance to recalibrate. This is the beauty of the "Decide and See How You Feel" method: it gives you permission to try, learn, and pivot without feeling stuck.

This isn't about being reckless—it's about curiosity. It's about starting with grace and trusting yourself to figure out things as you go.

One of my favorite decision-making strategies is simple: make a choice and pay attention to how you feel afterward. Does making that choice fill you with excitement or a sense of relief? Or does it leave you feeling unsettled, like something isn't quite right? This method has helped me navigate everything from career choices to personal projects.

Reflection Questions

1. What's one decision you've been putting off because you don't feel ready?

2. How can you create a safety net for yourself to make starting less intimidating?
3. Think of a time when you started something before you felt fully prepared. What did you learn from that experience?

Action Steps

- Identify one thing you've been hesitant to start and take a small step toward it this week.
- Practice the "decide and see how you feel" method with a low-stakes decision, like choosing a restaurant or trying a new hobby.
- Reflect on a past decision that didn't go as planned. What did you learn, and how can you apply that lesson moving forward?

Starting isn't about having all the answers. It's about taking that first, sometimes messy, step and trusting that the path will reveal itself as you go. Fear of failure will always linger, but so will the chance for success. You won't know what's possible until you take that first step.

CHAPTER 5

Getting Your Message Out There

As nurses, we often think about how to get critical information to the right people. Whether it's the latest research or essential public health advice, the challenge is always the same: how do we make it accessible, actionable, and impactful? For years, the traditional paths—academic journals and conferences—have been the go-to, but those channels have limits. They're inaccessible to most bedside nurses and nearly invisible to the public. If you want to truly make an impact, you have to meet people where they are.

The Limits of Traditional Dissemination

Let's talk about journals and conferences. They're valuable in their own right—peer-reviewed articles provide credibility and conferences foster professional networking—but let's be real. Most nurses don't have time to read journal articles during their shifts or attend multi-day conferences. Many are juggling 12-hour shifts, family responsibilities, and tight budgets. Even if you wanted to attend, the cost of registration, travel, and time off can be prohibitive.

In school, we're taught how to navigate academic databases, find a DOI (Digital Object Identifier), and analyze research papers. But let's be honest: in clinical practice, those skills often gather dust. The reality is that most bedside nurses aren't turning to academic journals for information—they're relying on what's readily available and practical for their daily work.

This disconnect means the majority of the nursing workforce never sees the innovative practices and best practices being shared in academic circles. The result? A massive gap in translating knowledge into practice.

The Power of Social Media

Here's the thing: the frustration over people getting their news from social media isn't entirely misplaced. It can feel chaotic and unreliable at times. But social media also represents a massive opportunity. Instead of lamenting where people get their information, we should focus on meeting them there and providing content that's accurate, engaging, and actionable.

Sharing on social media doesn't mean uploading a screenshot of a journal article and hoping someone reads it. Nobody's going to. It means simplifying complex ideas into plain language, using visuals that capture attention, and creating content that sparks curiosity. Nurses have a unique ability to bridge the gap between research and the public, but only if we embrace these new tools.

Consider the *Walking Home from the ICU* podcast by nurse practitioner Kali Dayton. Through her episodes, she shares evidence-based practices like getting ventilated patients up and walking early to improve outcomes. But it's her use of short-form video on social media—showing patients walking while still on ventilators—that grabs attention and drives the message home. These videos make the science visible, digestible, and real. They reach not just clinicians but also patients and their families, fostering change at every level.

Why Sound Bites Matter More Than Journal Articles

Let's be clear: journal articles have their place, but they aren't enough. A catchy sound bite or a 30-second video can convey an idea faster than a 5,000-word paper. For example, the FAST acronym for recognizing stroke symptoms (Facial drooping, Arm weakness, Speech difficulty, Time to call 911) has saved countless lives—not because it was buried in a journal, but because it was distilled into a simple, memorable message that could be shared widely.

Nurses are perfectly positioned to create these sound bites. We already translate complex medical jargon into patient-friendly language every day. By applying those same skills to social media or podcasting, we can amplify critical information and make it accessible to a much broader audience.

A Case Study: Stronger After Stroke

Take the *Stronger After Stroke* podcast. This project started as a way to share interviews with neurologists, rehab specialists, and stroke survivors. To promote it, my organization encouraged me to use social media. Without ads, gatekeepers, or mainstream media, the podcast has reached listeners in over 86 countries. It won first place at the International Stroke Conference for the American Heart Association in 2024. And now providers all over the world recommend it to their patients and caregivers as a resource for recovery.

Social media made this possible. It cut through the bureaucracy and allowed the message to reach those who needed it most. And it proved to me that nurses can use these tools to fill gaps in public health messaging in ways that traditional systems simply can't.

Practical Tips for Getting Your Message Out

So how can you get your message out there? Here are some practical steps:

1. **Know your audience.** Are you trying to reach patients, other healthcare professionals, or the general public? Tailor your tone and content accordingly.
2. **Simplify your message.** Focus on one key takeaway. If you're explaining a new procedure, break it down into a single, actionable idea.
3. **Use visuals.** Videos, infographics, and even simple images can make complex concepts much easier to grasp.
4. **Create hooks.** Start with a question or surprising fact to grab attention. For example: "Did you know early mobilization for ICU patients can cut hospital stays in half?"
5. **Be consistent.** Building an audience takes time. Post regularly and engage with comments and questions to foster a sense of community.

Expanding Public Health Messaging

The importance of public health messaging has never been clearer. Whether it's encouraging vaccinations, promoting mental health resources, or addressing social determinants of health like loneliness, nurses are uniquely equipped to lead these conversations.

I've also seen this in my work with the *Aging Like a Pro* podcast, where we focus on translating aging-related research into actionable advice. Through simple, relatable language and engaging discussions, we've reached listeners who otherwise wouldn't have access to these resources. It's another example of how we can take what we know and make it matter to more people.

Reflection Questions

1. Where do your patients or peers currently get their information? How can you make it easier for them to access credible resources?
2. What's one complex idea you could distill into a simple, engaging sound bite?
3. Think about a time when you learned something valuable from a non-traditional source. How did that impact you?

Action Steps

1. Choose one key message you want to share. Write it out in one sentence, and then think of a visual or example to bring it to life.
2. Create a short video, infographic, or social media post about that message. Share it and track how people engage with it.
3. Explore podcasts, blogs, or social media accounts in your field for inspiration on how others are disseminating their messages effectively.

Getting your message out there isn't about doing things the way they've always been done. It's about meeting people where they are, sharing what matters in a way they can understand, and empowering them to take action. As nurses, we're already experts at this. The only question is: what's your message, and how will you share it?

CONCLUSION

The Power of Starting Now

As we reach the end of this book, I want you to remember something: your voice holds immense power. It's not just about the stories you tell or the insights you share—it's about the connections you forge and the change you inspire. Whether you're speaking to colleagues, patients, or a broader audience, your impact extends far beyond what you can see.

Throughout my journey from ICU nurse to podcaster and advocate, I've learned that the most powerful credential isn't another degree or certification—it's experience. Those eight years in the ICU, the countless patient interactions, the challenges we faced and overcame—these aren't just memories. They're expertise earned through real-world experience, and they're worth sharing.

Think about the knowledge you've gained in your career. The workarounds you've discovered, the processes you've improved, the patients whose lives you've touched. Each of these experiences has shaped your unique perspective, and that perspective matters. The healthcare system needs your voice now, not after you've earned another credential or reached some arbitrary milestone of "readiness."

Remember my "decide and see how you feel" method? That same approach applies here. Take that first step, notice how it feels, and adjust as needed. You don't need permission to make an impact. You don't need to wait until everything feels perfect. Start where you are, with what you know, and let your impact grow from there.

Your experiences—every challenging shift, every difficult conversation, every problem you've solved—have prepared you for this moment. The world needs your perspective, your insights, and your willingness to show up as yourself. Whether it's through podcasting, speaking, writing, or advocating, your voice can create ripples of change that extend far beyond what you can currently imagine.

I've built my platform by focusing on authenticity and connection, sharing what I've learned through my journey from bedside nurse to podcaster and advocate. Now, I help others do the same through speaking engagements, consulting, and media projects. If you're ready to amplify your voice and build your platform, I'm here to help you take that next step.

Remember: The permission you're waiting for doesn't exist. Your time to act is now. Press start.

Connect with me on NurseRosaSpeaks.com or connect with me on social media @NurseRosaSpeaks

www.ingramcontent.com/pod-product-compliance
Lightning Source LLC
LaVergne TN
LVHW021328100326
833349LV00008B/113